Best Underdog Stories in Sports

Michelle Shalton

Series Editor
Jeffrey D. Wilhelm

Much thought, debate, and research went into choosing and ranking the 10 items in each book in this series. We realize that everyone has his or her own opinion of what is most significant, revolutionary, amazing, deadly, and so on. As you read, you may agree with our choices, or you may be surprised — and that's the way it should be!

an imprint of

SCHOLASTIC

www.scholastic.com/librarypublishing

A Rubicon book published in association with Scholastic Inc.

Rubicon © 2008 Rubicon Publishing Inc.
www.rubiconpublishing.com

Associate Publishers: Kim Koh, Miriam Bardswich
Project Editor: Amy Land
Editor: Jessica Calleja
Creative Director: Jennifer Drew
Project Manager/Designer: Jeanette MacLean
Graphic Designer: Andrea Jankun

The publisher gratefully acknowledges the following for permission to reprint copyrighted material in this book.

Every reasonable effort has been made to trace the owners of copyrighted material and to make due acknowledgment. Any errors or omissions drawn to our attention will be gladly rectified in future editions.

"Jim Abbott Remembers" (excerpt from "Jim Abbott: former left-hand pitcher recalls his 1993 no-hitter against the Cleveland Indians at Yankee Stadium") by Al Doyle. From *Baseball Digest* magazine, May 1, 2007. Reprinted courtesy of *Baseball Digest*.

"25 years ago, they changed history" (excerpt) by Jim Kelley for ESPN.com, originally published December 8, 2005, on ESPN.com.

"The Little Guy with a Big Dream" (excerpt) from www.rudyinternational.com. Reprinted with permission.

Cover image: Olympic Gymnastics–Photo by Doug Pensinger/Getty Images

Library and Archives Canada Cataloguing in Publication

Shalton, Michelle
      The 10 best underdog stories in sports / Michelle Shalton.

Includes index.
ISBN: 978-1-55448-495-9

      1. Readers (Elementary). 2. Readers—Sports.
I. Title. II. Title: Ten best underdog stories in sports.

PE1117.S4355 2007   428.6   C2007-906859-6

1 2 3 4 5 6 7 8 9 10   10   17 16 15 14 13 12 11 10 09 08

489 004 4

Printed in Singapore

Contents

ANYTHING IS POSSIBLE

Have you ever heard the fable about the race between the tortoise and the hare? No one thought the tortoise stood a chance. "He's way too slow!" everyone thought. "He's crazy for even trying!" they said. Everyone saw the tortoise as a major underdog. No one believed in him. But somehow, the slow moving tortoise found a way to overcome the odds and beat the speedy hare. It shocked everyone. That is, everyone except the tortoise, who believed that he could win from the very start.

There have been many inspirational underdog stories in the annals of sports history. In this book, we take a look at the 10 most inspiring stories.

When ranking these stories, we considered the following criteria: Did the story feature athletes who had to overcome seemingly impossible odds? Did the story help people believe that anything is possible? Did it inspire other athletes to pursue their dreams? How long has the underdog story endured? Was it captivating enough to be retold in movies, books, and articles?

It's time to cheer for the underdog! As you read, ask yourself:

annals: *records; archives*

WHO IS THE MOST INSPIRATIONAL SPORTS UNDERDOG OF ALL TIME?

⑩ MANON RHÉA

Manon Rhéaume goaltending for the Tampa Bay Lightning

SPORT: Hockey

ONE SHINING MOMENT: First woman to play in the National Hockey League (NHL)

GOING THE DISTANCE: Inspired female athletes to "dream big"

Manon Rhéaume (Maa-nohn Ray-ohm) didn't have to wait long for the first shot. It was snapped from just inside the blue line — hard and fast. She reacted instantly to deflect it. Then came another and another. Less than two minutes into the game, she faced three shots and blocked them all. When the period was over, she had faced nine shots and stopped seven of them. More important, she had made history.

On September 23, 1992, in a preseason exhibition game between the Tampa Bay Lightning and the St. Louis Blues, 20-year-old Rhéaume skated onto the ice and straight into history. By goaltending for the Lightning, she had become the first woman to play hockey in the NHL. In fact, she had become the first woman to play in any of the four major sports leagues in North America.

After the game, people had strong opinions about her NHL debut. *Sports Illustrated* called it a "sideshow." Others saw it as a groundbreaking achievement. Despite the different opinions, Rhéaume's story became an inspiration not only for young women, but for people everywhere.

---

blue line: *one of two blue lines that divide the rink into three equal zones (offensive, defensive, and neutral)*
period: *one of three 20 minute playing intervals with a break in between each interval*
debut: *first appearance*

 What do you think *Sports Illustrated* meant by "sideshow"? Do you think it was a fair way to describe the event? Why or why not?

MANON RHÉAUME

AGAINST THE ODDS

Manon Rhéaume was born in February 1972. Growing up in Quebec, Canada, she laced up her first pair of skates at the age of three. By the time she was five, her hockey-mad brothers were dressing her up as a goalie to fire shots at her in their backyard rink. With very few girls' leagues to choose from, it wasn't long before Rhéaume was playing on boys' teams. From the start, she faced injuries, insults, sexism, and countless doubters. But she was determined to overcome the discrimination and the odds stacked against her. At the age of 11, she became the first girl to play in Quebec's International Pee Wee Hockey Tournament. By the time she was 19, she was playing for the Trois-Rivieres Draveurs, one of Quebec's junior men's hockey teams.

GLORY DAYS

All of Rhéaume's hard work was rewarded the moment she skated onto the ice to tend goal for the Tampa Bay Lightning. But the end of that game wasn't the end of Rhéaume's professional hockey career. She went on to become the first woman to play in a regular season professional men's hockey game with the Atlanta Knights of the International Hockey League. She would also play one more exhibition game for the Lightning the following season. Rhéaume continued to play in the men's minor leagues for Las Vegas, Knoxville, Nashville, and Charlotte.

INSPIRING LEGACY

Rhéaume was one of the first women to challenge hockey's gender stereotypes. After her famous NHL debut, women's hockey became an Olympic sport. Rhéaume's groundbreaking career also helped to pave the way for other talented young women. Rhéaume is now a coach and a designer of hockey equipment. She continues to inspire multitudes of women to step onto the ice and follow her example.

Quick Fact

As a young girl, Rhéaume also danced ballet, skied, and played baseball. But as she once told a reporter, "I didn't just play hockey. It was my passion."

Rhéaume at a news conference following her first game with the Tampa Bay Lightning

? Why do you think it's important to be passionate? Think about something in your life that you are passionate about and explain why it makes you feel that way.

The Expert Says...

"Rhéaume helped bring women's hockey to the big time. At the time, hockey was not an Olympic sport for women. Now it is."

— Kara Yorio, NHL columnist, *The Sporting News*

10   9   8   7   6

She's Got GAME!

Manon Rhéaume didn't mean to become the poster girl for women's hockey. She simply wanted to play with the best. These biographical accounts detail some of her experiences as the only girl in a boy's game.

When Rhéaume was six years old, she began playing on a boy's team that her father coached. Her father didn't want people to know she was a girl because he wanted to make sure she was judged on her skill alone. So he made her suit up at home before games and practices and put on her helmet in the parking lot.

When she was 11 years old, Rhéaume was on her way to play for a boy's Pee Wee team. Her brother accidentally shut the car door on one of her hands, leaving her fingers blue, swollen, and bruised. Through tears she insisted on playing, and did.

Rhéaume broke her left leg skiing when she was eight years old. But she didn't let that keep her off the ice! She kept playing hockey with her brothers, keeping one leg in a goalie pad and the other in a cast.

While playing her first game with the Trois-Rivieres Draveurs, a slapshot shattered Rhéaume's face mask, cutting her eye. Bleeding all over her face and jersey, she stuck it out on the ice until play stopped.

slapshot: *powerful shot on goal generated by a full swing of the hockey stick*

Canada's Manon Rhéaume goaltending at the 1998 Nagano Winter Olympics

? Rhéaume has played with swollen fingers, a broken leg, and a bleeding eye. In many cases, she had to be even tougher than the boys to be taken half as seriously on the ice. Do you think this was fair? Why or why not?

Take Note

Manon Rhéaume's pioneering actions put her into the #10 spot on our list. She faced an uphill battle her entire hockey career, simply because she was a girl. She made history when she played in the NHL, and proved her critics wrong with her tough attitude, determined spirit, and passion for the game.

- Rhéaume's courage inspired other young girls to step out onto the ice. Do you think it's important for athletes to inspire others? Why or why not?

5   3   2   1

9 JIM ABBOTT

Jim Abbott pitches at Yankee Stadium.

JIM ABBOTT—PHOTO BY RONALD C. MODRA/SPORTS IMAGERY/GETTY IMAGES

SPORT: Baseball

ONE SHINING MOMENT: Pitched a no-hitter against the Cleveland Indians

GOING THE DISTANCE: Overcame a physical disability to play Major League Baseball

When Carlos Baerga hit a grounder to Randy Velarde for the final out of the game, the crowd cheered wildly. On September 4, 1993, Jim Abbott, a pitcher for the New York Yankees, accomplished what every major league pitcher dreams about, but very few achieve — a no-hitter. He did it against the Cleveland Indians, a team loaded with talented hitters. And he did it while pitching for one of the oldest and most successful teams in baseball — the New York Yankees.

In baseball, pitching an entire game without allowing a single hit from the opposing team is a remarkable accomplishment at any level of play. Only nine other Yankees have ever pitched a no-hitter. In Abbott's case, it was even more incredible because he only has one hand.

For Abbott the athlete, the no-hitter was a major accomplishment in a successful baseball career. For millions of people, Abbott's achievement is proof that with determination, hard work, and belief in oneself, anything is possible.

grounder: *batted baseball that rolls along the ground*

JIM ABBOTT

AGAINST THE ODDS

Jim Abbott was born in September 1967 in Michigan. Born without a right hand, his rise to the major leagues is an amazing story. Abbott discovered his love of baseball at an early age and spent hours practicing his throwing and catching by bouncing a ball off the wall. He would keep his glove on the end of his right arm and pitch with his left. After delivering his pitch, he would quickly switch the glove from his right arm to his left hand to catch any balls that bounced back to him.

> ? Abbott learned his glove-switching method while playing catch as a young boy with his father. He was constantly practicing to improve his method. Which do you think is more important — natural talent or practice? Explain.

Quick Fact

In high school, Abbott also played football. He was the starting quarterback and led his school's team to the finals of the Michigan state championship. He says he preferred baseball because "it was just the sport I was best at."

Yankee Stadium first opened in 1923 and can hold almost 60,000 people.

The Expert Says...

" We tend to take him for granted, but that doesn't mean what he does isn't amazing. We'll probably never see another like him. "

— Marcel Lachemann, California Angels pitching coach

GLORY DAYS

After graduating from high school, Abbott accepted a baseball scholarship from the University of Michigan. In his three years at Michigan, he led the Wolverines to two Big Ten titles. In 1987, Abbott pitched the U.S. to a silver medal at the Pan-American Games. He also pitched the last game of the 1988 Summer Olympics to help the U.S. take gold. The California Angels signed him in 1989. He became one of the rare players who jumped from college to the majors without spending time in the minor leagues. Abbott rewarded their confidence by winning 12 games his first season. His best year came in 1991 with 18 wins. His most memorable game will always be the no-hitter he pitched against the Indians in 1993.

INSPIRING LEGACY

Abbott overcame a major obstacle on his road to success. He did not allow his disability to define him. As he says, "There are millions of people out there ignoring disabilities and accomplishing incredible feats. I learned you can learn to do things differently, but do them just as well." Today, Jim Abbott is a motivational speaker reaching out to people all over the world with his incredible story.

Big Ten: *alliance of 11 large universities located in the Midwest — Ohio State, Illinois, Michigan, Wisconsin, Penn State, Iowa, Purdue, Michigan State, Indiana, Northwestern, Minnesota*

Quick Fact

Abbott showed so much early promise as a pitcher that the Toronto Blue Jays selected him straight out of high school in the 36th round of the 1985 draft. He decided to go to college at the University of Michigan instead of signing a contract with Toronto.

Jim Abbott Remembers

**A personal memoir from *Baseball Digest*
As told to Al Doyle, May 1, 2007**

My no-hitter against the Indians at Yankee Stadium on September 4, 1993, is one game I'll never forget. ...

The Indians had a very tough lineup with guys like Kenny Lofton, Carlos Baerga, Albert Belle, and Manny Ramirez, and I was wild early in the game. The first pitch I threw would have been a wild pitch if someone had been on base. There may have been some jitters about wanting to do better than I did in the game before.

Even though I wasn't striking guys out — there were only three strikeouts in the game — I had a good fastball. Guys were hitting grounders and pop-ups on inside fastballs, and I used a lot of off-speed pitches. The curveball was good that night. ...

The Yankees were still in the [playoff] race, so I was focused on getting guys out and winning rather than thinking about a no-hitter. The fans really started getting into it in the sixth or seventh inning. Even though it wasn't a huge crowd (27,125), it sounded like the stadium was full. The crowd seemed bigger than it was. ...

I was focusing on working with Matt Nokes behind the plate, trying to zero in and throw quality pitches. I'll be the first to admit it. My knees were knocking in the ninth inning. I've seen the tape of the game, and I looked a lot calmer than I was. ...

When the final out was made, it was like time slowed down. It was like someone hit a mute button, then the sound was turned on loud. ...

? Abbott uses many baseball terms in this article — wild pitch, strikeout, fastball, grounder, pop-up, off-speed pitch, curveball. If you are not familiar with the terms, find out what they mean.

Take Note

Jim Abbott's determination places him at #9 on our list. He was a courageous athlete who beat the odds and proved that, no matter what the circumstances, it is possible to accomplish incredible achievements. He is an inspiration not only to people with disabilities, but to anyone who must overcome great obstacles.
• Abbott received tremendous encouragement as a young boy. He once said that many people believed in him, even when he didn't believe in himself. How do you think a strong support system helps people to succeed?

Houston and North Carolina State players battle for a rebound during the NCAA championship game.

SPORT: Basketball

ONE SHINING MOMENT: The underestimated Wolfpack stunned the basketball world by defeating the top-ranked team to win the National Collegiate Athletic Association (NCAA) championship.

GOING THE DISTANCE: Showed other underdogs that anything is possible no matter what the odds

"One desperation heave. One dunk. One miracle." That's how *The Sporting News* summed up one of the most remarkable college basketball games ever played. On April 4, 1983, in Albuquerque, New Mexico, the underdog North Carolina (NC) State Wolfpack faced off against the top-ranked Houston Cougars in the NCAA championship game. With the score tied at 52 – 52 and just a few seconds left on the clock, the Wolfpack's Derek Whittenburg heaved a desperation shot from over 29 feet away. It was short of the rim, but Whittenburg's teammate Lorenzo Charles was right under the basket waiting for the rebound. With one second left, Charles leaped, caught the ball, and slammed it through the rim to give the Wolfpack a 54 – 52 win.

Charles's game-winning dunk triggered a frenzy. Wolfpack coach Jim Valvano ran onto the court in shock, searching for someone to hug. No one had expected Valvano's "Cardiac Pack," as they were called, to even compete with the strong and athletic Cougars, nicknamed "Phi Slama Jama." Not only did the Wolfpack compete, they won the NCAA championship in historic fashion, inspiring basketball fans and players everywhere.

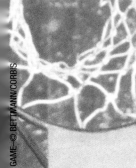

BASKETBALL GAME—© BETTMANN/CORBIS

1983 NORTH CAROLINA STATE WOLFPACK

AGAINST THE ODDS

NC State finished the 1983 season with 10 losses. The only chance they had to qualify for the NCAA championship tournament was to win the Atlantic Coast Conference (ACC) tournament. The Houston Cougars were college basketball's team to beat. Loaded with talented stars such as Hakeem Olajuwon and Clyde Drexler, they were ranked #1 in the country. Houston was picked by nearly every expert to easily win the title, but NC State wasn't even expected to advance past its first-round game.

Quick Fact

The Cougars were so sure they would beat the Wolfpack that they didn't put much effort into pre-title game practices. The team's coach, Guy Lewis, knew his players were being lazy. So the night before the game, he ordered them to the hotel and enforced a curfew.

 How do you think the Cougars' overconfident attitude worked to the Wolfpack's advantage?

NC State coach Jim Valvano (far right) celebrates with his team after winning the national title.

GLORY DAYS

The Wolfpack and the Cougars found themselves face to face on April 4, 1983. They had followed very different paths to get to the national championship game. The Cougars had blown out every team they faced. The Wolfpack had narrowly beaten almost every team to get there.

The Cougars were known for their exciting, explosive dunks. The Wolfpack countered by packing their defenders close to the basket and playing patiently on offense. When Lorenzo Charles made his famous last-second dunk, he pulled off one of basketball's most shocking upsets.

INSPIRING LEGACY

The Wolfpack's victory continues to be an inspiration for every underdog that is selected to play in the NCAA championship tournament. Now every team that qualifies for the NCAA tournament believes they have a chance to win the title, no matter how low they are ranked or how much they have struggled. Wolfpack team member Thurl Bailey couldn't believe the effect that game had on people, "They'd say watching us play inspired them to achieve more, to be better people. It taught a lesson about chasing your dreams."

blown out: *beaten by a huge margin*

Quick Fact

It was amazing that Wolfpack coach Jim Valvano was even able to coach the championship game. He was stricken by the flu and had a dangerously high fever. Valvano was so weak that trainer Jim Rehbock had to treat him with intravenous fluids before the game. Right after the game, Valvano went straight back to the hotel and to bed.

intravenous: *entering directly into a vein*

10   9   8   7   6

TWIST OF FATE

THE NC STATE WOLFPACK HAD TO OVERCOME THE ODDS TO GET TO THE NCAA CHAMPIONSHIP TOURNAMENT. THIS LIST RUNS THEM DOWN.

- No team with 10 losses had ever won the NCAA championship.

- During the regular season, the Wolfpack lost six times in one eight-game stretch. These included back-to-back 18-point losses to unranked teams.

- The Wolfpack trailed in the last minute of seven of their last nine wins.

- North Carolina beat Virginia in the postseason. They had lost to them twice during the regular season.

- The Wolfpack won their first-round tournament game against Pepperdine in overtime. With 24 seconds left on the clock, they came back from being six points behind.

- The Wolfpack needed to win the ACC tournament just to qualify for the NCAA tournament. Every game was a close call. They beat Wake Forest 71-70, North Carolina 91-84, and Virginia 81-78.

postseason: *after the regular season, the playoff tournaments to determine champions*

The Expert Says...

"Anybody needing to be inspired, anybody looking for a reason to believe, had to look no further than Valvano's never-say-die bunch of overachievers."

— Wayne Drehs, ESPN.com

Take Note

The North Carolina State Wolfpack takes the #8 spot on our list. Though Jim Abbott's achievement was a personal accomplishment, the entire Wolfpack squad came from behind to defeat the top-ranked team in college basketball. It was an upset that both shocked and inspired the sports world.

- Why do you think it's important for people to believe in themselves? Think of a time when you believed in yourself and overcame an obstacle. How did it make you feel?

5   4   3   2   1

7 VINCE PAPALE

Vince Papale (#83) runs upfield in a game against the New England Patriots.

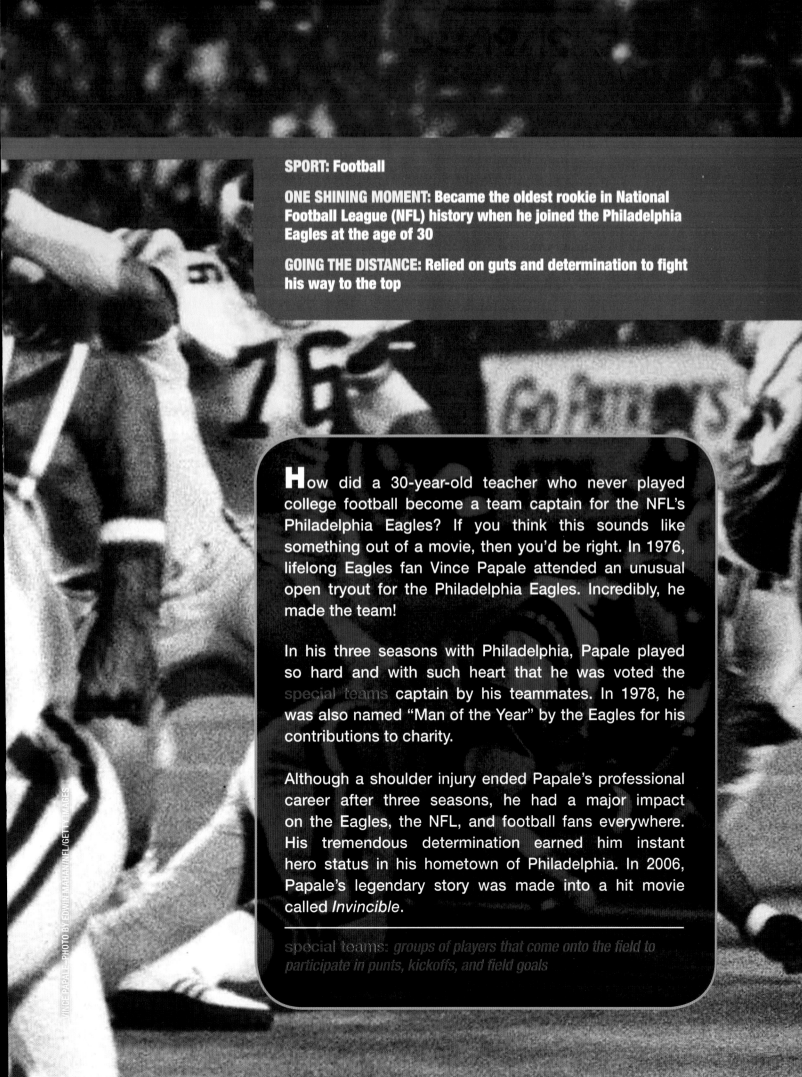

SPORT: Football

ONE SHINING MOMENT: Became the oldest rookie in National Football League (NFL) history when he joined the Philadelphia Eagles at the age of 30

GOING THE DISTANCE: Relied on guts and determination to fight his way to the top

How did a 30-year-old teacher who never played college football become a team captain for the NFL's Philadelphia Eagles? If you think this sounds like something out of a movie, then you'd be right. In 1976, lifelong Eagles fan Vince Papale attended an unusual open tryout for the Philadelphia Eagles. Incredibly, he made the team!

In his three seasons with Philadelphia, Papale played so hard and with such heart that he was voted the special teams captain by his teammates. In 1978, he was also named "Man of the Year" by the Eagles for his contributions to charity.

Although a shoulder injury ended Papale's professional career after three seasons, he had a major impact on the Eagles, the NFL, and football fans everywhere. His tremendous determination earned him instant hero status in his hometown of Philadelphia. In 2006, Papale's legendary story was made into a hit movie called *Invincible*.

special teams: *groups of players that come onto the field to participate in punts, kickoffs, and field goals*

VINCE PAPALE · PHOTO BY EDWIN MAHAN/NFL/GETTY IMAGES

VINCE PAPALE

AGAINST THE ODDS

Vince Papale was born in February 1946 in Pennsylvania. In high school, Papale excelled in track, basketball, and football. Because of his small size, he decided to focus on track and ended up playing only one year of high-school football. When Papale graduated from high school, he was too small for college football, so he went to Philadelphia's St. Joseph's University on a full track scholarship. By the time he graduated, Papale had sprouted to 6'2" and weighed 185 pounds. But he never played football because St. Joseph's didn't have a team. In 1974, he tried out for the Philadelphia Bell of the World Football League. Papale made the team, but the franchise folded after one year.

Quick Fact

Before Papale tried out for the Eagles, he played in Philadelphia's "rough touch" leagues. He broke his nose, fractured some ribs, and had a few teeth jarred loose. Papale remembers the games as more "rough" than "touch" with an ambulance always nearby in case anyone got injured.

Vince Papale in 2006

GLORY DAYS

When Dick Vermeil started out as head coach of the Philadelphia Eagles, he wanted to shake things up. To do this, he held an open tryout, allowing anyone who showed up to participate. Many people thought he was crazy. No one believed he would ever find someone good enough to make the team. Vermeil was just as surprised as anyone else when he came across Papale, "When we saw him and how bad he wanted it, we said, 'Hey, this guy's worth a shot.'" At first, the rest of the players weren't thrilled with an outsider joining their team. But Papale kept quiet and worked hard every day. His determination and selfless play eventually won over his teammates, and he was voted special teams captain.

> How do you think Papale felt being a new player on a professional football team? Think of some ways team members can make a newcomer feel welcome.

INSPIRING LEGACY

Despite playing only three seasons in the NFL, Papale's love for the game, his work ethic, and his against-all-odds story inspired people everywhere. The release of the movie *Invincible* in 2006 shone the spotlight on Papale's incredible life story. In the years since his NFL playing days, Papale has been a motivational speaker. He has beaten colon cancer and is now a spokesperson for the prevention of the disease. In short, Papale continues to inspire those around him with the same qualities that made him an unlikely, but much loved, NFL hero.

7

6

INVINCIBLE!

Papale's story was made into a hit movie called *Invincible*. This report explains how the movie came to be.

In November 2002, the NFL honored the 25th anniversary of the classic movie *Rocky* by airing a report about it on ESPN during Monday Night Football. *Rocky* is about an unknown boxer from Philadelphia who gets a once-in-a-lifetime shot at the heavyweight championship.

Along with the anniversary piece, a similar report ran about a real-life *Rocky* story that featured Papale. After the show aired, Papale started getting calls from Hollywood. One thing led to another, and soon a film was in the works. Actor Mark Wahlberg was cast to play Papale. Papale was involved in the movie every step of the way. He was even on the set almost every day during filming. When the movie came out, it was in the top spot at the box office for two weeks in a row.

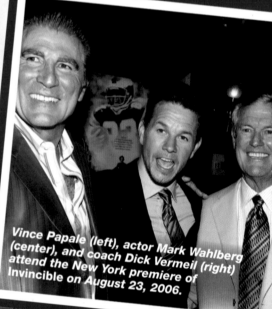

Vince Papale (left), actor Mark Wahlberg (center), and coach Dick Vermeil (right) attend the New York premiere of *Invincible* on August 23, 2006.

Quick Fact

Papale and Wahlberg became good friends during the filming of *Invincible*. Papale thought Wahlberg's performance was phenomenal, once commenting, "He plays me better than I do."

? How do you think their friendship would have helped Wahlberg deliver a more accurate performance in the film?

The Expert Says...

"It all just fit. He ran [100 yards in 4.5 seconds], caught the ball well, and made the team. He just had a passion to play the game.

— Dick Vermeil, Papale's coach with the Philadelphia Eagles

Take Note

Vince Papale's story of determination puts him at #7 on our list. The Wolfpack players were in their prime when they won the NCAA championship title. Papale thought his professional football days were over. Through an unexpected twist of fate, he went from teaching to a professional NFL career. By taking hold of a unique opportunity, he proved that even the toughest odds can be overcome.
• What do you find especially inspiring about Vince Papale's story? Explain.

5   4   3   2   1

6 1988 JAMAICAN

Jamaican bobsled pilot, Dudley Stokes, jumps in as his three teammates push off at the start of the second run of the four-man event on February 27, 1988.

BOBSLED TEAM

SPORT: Bobsled

ONE SHINING MOMENT: Despite a last-place finish, their determination and courage won the hearts of fans and the respect of fellow competitors.

GOING THE DISTANCE: They were the first Jamaican team to ever compete in the Winter Olympic Games.

The 1988 Winter Olympics were held in Calgary, Canada. The world was surprised to see Jamaica — an island nation that has never seen snow — enter a team to compete in the bobsled competition. Although short on experience, the Jamaican team captured the hearts of millions of fans around the world with one of the most inspiring and sensational last-place performances ever seen.

The team faced injuries, technical difficulties, crashes, and many doubters. In the third heat of the four-man bobsled event, the Jamaican team flew out to the seventh-fastest start, but ended their race with a spectacular crash. Despite this accident, the Jamaicans' teamwork, passion, and dedication earned them the respect of both fans and fellow competitors. Their courageous debut into the sport of bobsledding inspired later Jamaican bobsled teams to follow in their footsteps.

heat: *opening race that decides which teams move on to the final race*

1988 JAMAICAN BOBSLED TEAM

AGAINST THE ODDS

It started with two Americans, George Fitch and William Maloney, who thought of the idea after watching a pushcart competition in Jamaica. In bobsledding, a strong start is needed to gain speed, and this requires powerful sprinters. Jamaica is known for producing some of the best sprinters in the world, so Fitch and Maloney went recruiting there. They first approached a few of Jamaica's Olympic sprinters, but none were interested. So they took their idea to the military and, after a series of tryouts, the first Jamaican bobsled team was formed. The members of the 1988 Olympic team were Lieutenant Devon Harris, Private Michael White, Captain Dudley Stokes, and his brother Chris Stokes.

pushcart: *cart with a shallow box body and wheels; one person sits in the cart to steer and another pushes to get it rolling*
sprinters: *athletes who run short distances at top speed*

Quick Fact

Chris Stokes joined the team late because of an injury to an original team member. He had less than one week of bobsled training before competing at the Olympics.

GLORY DAYS

With limited training and little experience, the Jamaican bobsled team found themselves competing against some of the best bobsledders in the world. Their first two heats were full of technical mistakes. Yet they stayed positive and worked hard to improve. Their third heat is now legendary. The Jamaican team shocked everyone by pushing the seventh-fastest start time, but sadly ended up crashing halfway into the course. The team may have finished in last place, but they were celebrated worldwide for their sportsmanship and determination.

INSPIRING LEGACY

Many people thought Jamaica's 1988 bobsled team was a joke, but the team proved their critics wrong. In 1994, they stunned the world in Lillehammer, Norway, when their four-man team placed 14th, above the Russian, French, Italian, and U.S. teams. The Jamaican team had the fastest start in the two-man event at the 2002 Salt Lake City Winter Olympics. And it all started with the 1988 Olympic team. Their inspiring story paved the way for future generations of Jamaican athletes. It also showed the world that a Caribbean nation can compete and succeed in a winter sport.

The story of the 1988 Jamaican bobsled team was turned into a 1993 comedy film titled Cool Runnings (pictured here).

6

ANATOMY OF A BOBSLED

This labeled photo breaks down the different parts that go into a successful four-man bobsled.

As the race starts, the **crewmen** push the bobsled for about 50 yards before jumping in. They have to create enough speed to move the sled through the rest of the race.

The **brakeman** pulls the brake lever after the bobsled crosses the finish line.

The **driver** is in charge of steering the bobsled. The driver pulls steering rings to change direction.

While pushing the bobsled, team members hold on to **push-bars** for support.

The fiberglass **hull** is closed in the front and open in the back.

Fixed pair of **rear runners**

The bobsled's **frame** is made out of steel.

Movable pair of **front runners**

Take Note

The 1988 Jamaican bobsled team takes the #6 spot. Vince Papale had at least played football before, but the Jamaican team was completely new to bobsledding. Many people thought it was impossible for a country that's famous for sun and sand to compete in a winter sport.
- The 1988 Jamaican bobsled team was the first from its country to ever compete in the Winter Olympics. How do you think the members of the Jamaican bobsled team felt, knowing that many people were expecting them to fail?

The Expert Says...

" There is an emotional connection between people and the Jamaican bobsled team. "

— Dudley Stokes, driver of the 1988 team and president of the Jamaican Bobsleigh Federation

5   4   3   2   1

5 KERRI STRUG

Kerri Strug sticks her gold medal-winning vault.

On July 23, 1996, the world witnessed one of the most dramatic finishes in Olympic history. The U.S. and Russian women's gymnastic teams were competing in the final day of team competition. The two talented teams were closely matched throughout the entire competition. The outcome came down to the last event on the final day.

After a dominating performance, the U.S. team had built a strong lead. But no one was sure whether it would be enough to clinch the gold medal. To be sure, the team needed one last strong performance on the final event — the vault. When U.S. gymnast Dominique Moceanu fell on both of her vaults, everyone believed the fate of the gold medal rested on the shoulders of her teammate Kerri Strug, who was the last person on the team to vault.

Fate took a nasty turn when Strug fell while landing her first attempt. As Strug tried to get up, everyone realized that it was more than just a bad fall — she had injured her ankle. As Strug limped back for her second vault it was obvious that she was in pain. Gathering determination, she flew down the runway and stuck her second vault on one leg. She raised her arms in victory, saluted the judges, and collapsed from the intense pain of her injury. The applause was deafening. Strug's incredible courage and poise made her an instant hero in the minds of athletes and fans around the world.

---

stuck: *executed a dismount or landing with such good technique that no extra steps are taken*

KERRI STRUG

AGAINST THE ODDS

Kerri Strug was born in November 1977 and grew up in Tucson, Arizona. Strug competed in her first meet when she was eight years old. She left home at 13 to train in Houston, Texas, with the world-famous gymnastics coach Bela Karolyi. Life in Karolyi's gym was tough, and Strug trained for eight hours almost every day. At the age of 14, she competed at the Barcelona Olympics and won a bronze medal. Karolyi retired soon after, and the next few years would be hard for Strug. During a 1994 competition, she slipped while performing on the uneven bars and severely pulled her back muscles. It was a very painful injury that took Strug six months to recover from. Later that same year, Karolyi came out of retirement and agreed to once again coach Strug. The next few years of competition would be her best.

meet: *athletic competition*

Quick Fact

Women's gymnastics is often criticized for being extremely demanding. Young female gymnasts are separated from loved ones, put on strict diets, and pushed to train for up to 12 hours a day (sometimes while injured). This lifestyle is especially challenging for young people whose minds and bodies are still developing.

Kerri Strug performs at an exhibition event on July 30, 1996.

GLORY DAYS

Until the 1996 Atlanta Olympics, Strug had lived in the shadow of her world-famous teammates. But when the team needed her, she did not let them down! After her first vault, she heard a pop and felt intense pain shoot through her ankle. As she limped back for her second vault, Karolyi encouraged her, "Kerri, listen to me. You can do it." Strug then landed the most famous vault of her career. Her one-footed landing earned her a score of 9.7 and sealed the U.S. team's victory. After the competition, it was discovered that she had torn two ligaments in her ankle.

? Find out about the events that gymnasts compete in. What physical and mental qualities does it take to be a champion gymnast?

INSPIRING LEGACY

Strug was always considered a supporting member on a star-studded U.S. team. Few people in the gymnastic world, including her own coach, believed she was talented enough to compete at the sport's highest levels. Strug's legendary vault changed everyone's mind. Strug put her career at risk by vaulting while seriously injured. Her sacrifice impressed people all over the world. Today, she travels the U.S. speaking to at-risk youth.

Quick Fact

Strug's courageous vault made her an instant celebrity in the United States. She made appearances on popular late-night talk shows, had a cameo on a hit television series, was pictured on the front of a cereal box, and met President Bill Clinton. Several magazines also featured Strug's dramatic landing on their covers.

cameo: *short appearance by a famous person*

10   9   8   7   6

BUMPY ROAD

Kerri Strug's career was filled with dramatic ups and downs. This list highlights some of her most memorable moments as an elite gymnast.

JANUARY 1991: Strug leaves home and heads to Bela Karolyi's Houston-based gym. She is 13 years old.

JUNE 1992: Strug competes in the trials for the Barcelona Olympics. She falls in the final round of the floor exercise. But she makes the team and is the youngest U.S. athlete at the 1992 Olympics.

LATE 1992: Strug is left without a coach when Karolyi announces his retirement after the 1992 Olympics. She spends three years bouncing from one coach to another.

AUGUST 1994: While competing at a small meet in Palm Springs, California, Strug slips on the uneven bars. She injures her back when she hits the mat. She needs six months of extensive rehabilitation.

LATE 1994: Karolyi comes out of retirement and agrees to once again coach Strug.

MARCH 1996: Strug wins the McDonald's American Cup gold medal, her first in an important competition.

JUNE 1996: Strug competes in the trials for the Atlanta Olympics. She earns the highest scores for two events and takes second place at the meet, earning her spot on the 1996 team.

JULY 1996: Strug makes history with her famous vault.

floor exercise: *event performed to music where the gymnast tumbles, leaps, and dances*

? Strug experienced many highs and lows throughout her gymnastic career, but refused to give up. What does this tell you about her personality?

The Expert Says...

" It was really a courageous performance in a crucial moment. "

— Bela Karolyi, 1996 U.S. coach

Take Note

Kerri Strug's story of determination takes the #5 spot on our list. The Jamaican bobsled team may have pioneered the sport for their country, but Strug risked her health and her career to help her team win the gold medal at the 1996 Olympics.
• How is Strug's athletic character reflected by her choice to put her team first?

5   4   3   2   1

James Braddock (left) fights Max Baer (right) on June 13, 1935, for the heavyweight championship title.

DOCK

ONE SHINING MOMENT: He defeated Max Baer to win the heavyweight championship of the world.

GOING THE DISTANCE: After hitting rock bottom, his remarkable comeback rekindled the hope of a country.

On the night of June 13, 1935, a 30-year-old boxer named James Braddock faced off against Max Baer, the reigning heavyweight champion of the world. Braddock, who had suffered numerous setbacks in his career, was a huge underdog against the seemingly unstoppable champ. Despite being considered past his prime, Braddock stepped into the ring. Most people didn't think he had a chance of winning, and many wondered whether he would even survive the fight.

Through 15 punishing rounds, the two fighters traded punch after punch. Braddock refused to go down despite absorbing many of the champ's crushing blows. When it was all over, both fighters were bruised and exhausted, but still standing. This meant that the winner would be chosen by judges. (During a match, boxing judges use a points system to keep track of how well each boxer fights.) The judges named Braddock the winner and he became the new heavyweight champion of the world.

Even though no one wanted to give him a chance in the ring, Braddock refused to give up. His victory over Baer is still remembered as one of the most spectacular upsets in sports history. This unlikely hero earned the nickname "Cinderella Man" because he proved just how hard a man would fight for his family and himself.

---

reigning: *holding a title*

JAMES BRADDOCK

AGAINST THE ODDS

James Braddock was born in June 1905 in New York City. He started boxing as a teenager and fought as an amateur before going professional in 1926. He had a successful early career defeating many strong fighters. But everything changed in 1929 when he lost an important title fight. The stock market crashed soon after, leading to the Great Depression. With no work available, Braddock struggled to support his family. To make matters worse, he shattered his powerful right hand in a fight and, unable to box, was forced to accept government money. But he never gave up, and his break came a few years later. Braddock beat two top-ranked boxers and earned a chance to fight for the title against heavyweight champion Max Baer.

amateur: *athlete who does not receive payment for competing*

Quick Fact

The Great Depression was an economic crisis that troubled North America and Europe throughout the 1930s. Banks and businesses collapsed, and millions of people lost their jobs.

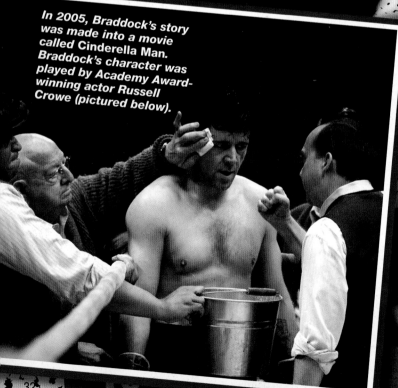

In 2005, Braddock's story was made into a movie called Cinderella Man. Braddock's character was played by Academy Award-winning actor Russell Crowe (pictured below).

GLORY DAYS

Before his championship fight with Baer, Braddock studied his opponent's boxing style. He figured he could win if he stayed away from Baer's powerful right punch, and that's just what he did. Braddock stunned the world when he won the fight and took the title. Two years later, at the age of 32, Braddock defended his heavyweight title against one of the greatest boxers of all time, Joe Louis. The much younger Louis took the title by knocking out Braddock in the eighth round. Braddock eventually hung up his gloves after a final win over Tommy Farr in 1938.

Quick Fact

Braddock's fight against Joe Louis was definitely a tough one. His only lucky punch was an uppercut that missed Louis's chin by an inch. Louis cut Braddock so badly that he needed 23 stitches after the fight. He also knocked a tooth into his lip. Braddock later said it felt like "someone jammed an electric bulb in my face and busted it. I couldn't have got up if they offered me a million dollars."

uppercut: *punch thrown upward into an opponent's chin*

? A few of the underdog stories in this book take place during difficult political or economic times. Why do you think this is?

INSPIRING LEGACY

Braddock's incredible comeback became a symbol of hope to millions of people during the Great Depression. He showed that anything is possible if a person never gives up. Braddock was voted into the Ring Boxing Hall of Fame in 1964, the Hudson County Hall of Fame in 1991, and the International Boxing Hall of Fame in 2001.

? What characteristics do you think an athlete must have to be voted into a hall of fame? Which of these characteristics do you think Braddock showed?

UP CLOSE WITH THE Champ

THIS PROFILE DETAILS JAMES BRADDOCK'S STATS AS A FIGHTER ...

Birth name: James Walter Braddock
Born: June 7, 1905
Died: November 29, 1974
Nickname: Cinderella Man
Division: Heavyweight
Height: 6'2 ½"
Weight: 193 lbs.
Reach: 75 in.
Total Fights: 85
Wins: 51
Knockouts: 26
Losses: 26
Draws: 7
Style: In his early career, a powerful right punch knocked out opponents in the early rounds of most fights. Never flashy, he was a systematic and determined fighter.

systematic: *efficient; methodical*

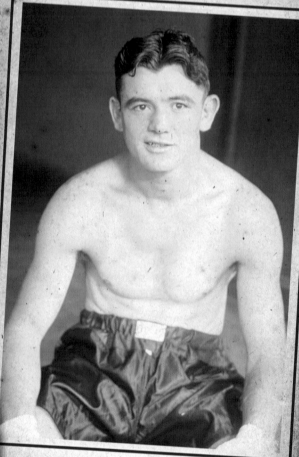

JAMES BRADDOCK IN 1929

The Expert Says ...

" [James Braddock] was the most courageous fighter I ever fought. "

— Joe Louis, heavyweight champion of the world from 1937 to 1949

Take Note

James Braddock takes the #4 spot on our list. Kerri Strug was an elite athlete with the best training. Braddock came out of nowhere to prove he was the best. Because of the high unemployment caused by the Great Depression, he was unable to provide for his family. It seemed like his boxing career was finished, but Braddock never let go of his determination and willed an impossible dream to come true.
• Why do you think Braddock's success gave so many people hope during the Great Depression?

5   **4**   3   2   1

Team USA celebrates their 4–3 victory over the Soviet team.

YMPIC HOCKEY TEAM

SPORT: Ice hockey

ONE SHINING MOMENT: This underestimated team of amateur and college players brought home the Olympic gold medal.

GOING THE DISTANCE: They had to defeat a legendary team in their quest for victory.

"Do you believe in miracles? YES!!!"

Sportscaster Al Michaels spoke these famous words at the end of the most spectacular upset in Olympic history. During round robin play at the 1980 Olympic Winter Games, Team USA came from behind to defeat the Soviet Union by a final score of 4–3. The next night, the Americans won the gold medal by coming from behind to beat Finland.

Team USA's win over the Soviet Union was a surprise victory. They entered the tournament ranked seventh out of the 12 teams. The Soviets were the top-ranked team and had beaten the Americans 10–3 just one week before the start of the Olympic Games. No one believed the Americans had a chance against the Soviets. Team USA was made up of a seemingly outmatched group of amateurs and college players, and the Soviet squad showcased some of hockey's most legendary names.

Team USA's victory has been described as the "most transcending moment" in the history of American hockey. It sent the country into a national celebration and made Team USA's players instant heroes.

round robin: *tournament in which each team plays every other team*
transcending: *going beyond the usual limits*

MEN'S HOCKEY TEAM · PHOTO BY STEVE POWELL/GETTY IMAGES

1980 U.S. MEN'S OLYMPIC HOCKEY TEAM

AGAINST THE ODDS

Team USA was made up of college players mixed with NHL hopefuls. Young players such as Mark Johnson, Neal Broten, Mark Pavelich, Ken Morrow, Dave Christian, and Mike Ramsey found themselves up against some of the best hockey teams in the world. They played a total of seven games and trailed in six of them! After their first game with Sweden ended in a 2 – 2 tie, Team USA surprised everyone by coming back to beat Czechoslovakia, Norway, Romania, and West Germany to earn a spot in the medal round. The first team they faced was the powerful Soviet squad. This face-off was set against the backdrop of the tense Cold War conflict between the United States and the Soviet Union.

Cold War: *period of military rivalry between the former Soviet Union and the United States following World War II*

Quick Fact

Solid goaltending by Team USA's Jim Craig was the extra boost the players needed to build their confidence. Craig stopped 36-of-39 shots throughout the game, including a furious storm of shots in the last 10 minutes.

? What qualities do you think it takes to be a good goaltender?

GLORY DAYS

The Americans were up against a legendary squad from a nation that had already won five gold medals for hockey. Boosted by support from the home crowd, Team USA kept the early part of the game close, trailing by one goal. But a goal by Johnson near the end of the first period evened the score at 2 – 2. After the first period, Soviet coach Viktor Tikhonov stunned everyone by pulling his star goalie, Vladislav Tretiak. At first, Tikhonov's strategy seemed to work as the Soviets regained the lead with a score of 3 – 2. But Team USA refused to go down without a fight. With about eight minutes left in the third period, Johnson scored his second goal to tie the game. Two minutes later, Team USA captain Mike Eruzione scored the winning goal.

INSPIRING LEGACY

Team USA's victory is remembered as the "Miracle on Ice." In 1980, the United States was dealing with several difficult situations — an American hostage crisis in Iran, high gas prices, inflation, and a Soviet invasion of Afghanistan, to name a few. It was difficult for Americans to find anything positive to hold on to. So when Team USA's young and energetic players began their gold-medal journey, they had the support of the entire nation.

inflation: *increase in prices; an individual dollar can buy less than it could before*

The Expert Says...

" We were just a bunch of talented, dedicated, wonderful guys who believed in one goal, and stuck all of our own personal ambitions away to achieve it. "

— Jim Craig, Team USA goalie

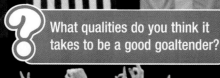

After they beat the Soviets, Team USA went on to play Finland for the gold medal. They beat Finland 4 – 2 to take the gold!

25 Years Ago, They Changed History

An article from ESPN.com, December 8, 2005

By Jim Kelley

A bunch of kids, handpicked by a virtually unknown coach, Herb Brooks, and Craig Patrick, now a general manager with Pittsburgh in the NHL, went to Lake Placid without a snowball's chance of winning. The Russians were the premier power. Even Brooks told his players that if they did everything perfectly and got most of the breaks, they were likely only to win a bronze medal, and that if they did everything perfectly and got all the breaks they could well win silver but that the gold, well, that belonged to the Russians, the best team in the world.

"He did say that," [Rob] McClanahan said. "He said it right before we opened against the Swedes, but then when he saw them he saw that they were flat and maybe complacent, and he realized that they were beatable and that there was an opportunity. ..."

With that in mind, Brooks drove his team, drove it exceptionally hard. The results paid off with what has been called a miracle.

"In some ways, what we accomplished wasn't really a miracle; it was the result of a coach with unbelievable passion who picked the right team and we executed his vision flawlessly," [Jim] Craig said. ...

"The thing that still amazes me is that 25 years later people remember what we did there and how it seemed to change things," Craig said, "and the most amazing thing of all is now that the movie has come out, there's a whole new generation of kids who are kind of seeing it the same way."

Quick Fact

This underdog story was turned into the 2004 Disney film *Miracle* starring Kurt Russell as coach Herb Brooks. The film is dedicated to Coach Brooks, who died in a car accident shortly after the film finished shooting.

? The players on the 1980 U.S. hockey team all worked together to achieve a common goal. How do you think teamwork helps a team to succeed?

Take Note

The 1980 U.S. Olympic men's team slides into the #3 spot. James Braddock had to defeat one man to prove his worth, but this team had to defeat a powerhouse squad. The "Miracle on Ice" tells the story of a determined and skilled group of amateur hockey players who pulled together to beat one of the world's most legendary teams. At a time of political tension between the Soviet Union and the U.S., the win was particularly uplifting for Americans.
• Do you think it is a good idea to mix sports and politics? Why or why not?

3

4   2   1

②SEABISCUIT

Seabiscuit and jockey, George Woolf, are in the lead.

SPORT: Horse racing

ONE SHINING MOMENT: Recovered from injury to beat the legendary racehorse known as War Admiral in the "Match of the Century"

GOING THE DISTANCE: Became one of the most celebrated racehorses of all time

On November 1, 1938, a small, awkward, knobby-kneed horse called Seabiscuit raced head-to-head against the much larger and more powerful Thoroughbred named War Admiral. War Admiral was a Triple Crown winner and a heavy favorite to win the race. No one other than Seabiscuit's loyal fans thought he had a chance.

At the sound of the starting bell, Seabiscuit charged into the lead. The 40,000 spectators, along with the 40 million people listening in on the radio, were on the edge of their seats. War Admiral eventually caught up to Seabiscuit on the backstretch. But Seabiscuit's jockey George Woolf — who was filling in for his injured friend Red Pollard — had a plan. He had slowed down Seabiscuit so the horse could see his competitor eye-to-eye. When that happened, Seabiscuit surged ahead, pulling away from War Admiral and winning the race by an amazing four lengths.

Although his improbable victory over War Admiral became the stuff of legend, it was only one small triumph in this incredible horse's life. Seabiscuit gave hope to millions during the Great Depression and captured the hearts of Americans long after his death.

Thoroughbred: *breed of racehorses descended from English mares and Arabian stallions*
Triple Crown: *very important racing competition that consists of three races for three-year-old Thoroughbred horses*
backstretch: *straight portion of the racetrack on the far side of the stands*
lengths: *measurements of a horse from nose to tail, usually about 8.2 feet*

SEABISCUIT

AGAINST THE ODDS

As a colt, Seabiscuit was undersized and knobby-kneed. He was considered lazy because he would eat and sleep for long periods of time. Seabiscuit's potential was overlooked because he didn't win many of his early races. Everything changed when he was bought by automobile entrepreneur Charles S. Howard. Tom Smith became his trainer and Red Pollard his jockey. Smith was patient and used new training techniques that calmed Seabiscuit so he could show his potential. Pollard also had an immediate connection with the horse. Together, they started winning races. Seabiscuit's fame spread as he continued to win throughout 1936 and 1937. Seabiscuit had only one rival, the imposing Thoroughbred named War Admiral, who had won all three races of the Triple Crown in 1937 and was voted "Horse of the Year."

---

colt: *young male horse under the age of four*
entrepreneur: *person who organizes and manages a business*

? Do you think it is important for a horse and rider to have a strong bond? How do you think this would affect their performance?

Jockey Red Pollard with Seabiscuit

GLORY DAYS

The much-anticipated race between Seabiscuit and War Admiral was called the "Match of the Century." After beating War Admiral, Seabiscuit was named 1938's "Horse of the Year." Not long after this victory, Seabiscuit badly injured his left leg in a race. Many people thought he would never race again. Around the same time, Pollard's leg was shattered in a riding accident, and many believed his career was also over. Both horse and rider slowly recovered together at Howard's California ranch. Incredibly, they attempted a racing comeback. After entering a few competitions, they signed up for the one race that had eluded them — the Santa Anita Handicap. Seabiscuit was trapped in third place as they entered the backstretch. Then a gap opened, and he surged to victory with a great burst of speed.

INSPIRING LEGACY

Seabiscuit inspired Americans who had been suffering from the terrible effects of the Great Depression. The horse that nobody wanted overcame adversity to become a great American champion. This incredible story continued to inspire millions with the release of the Oscar-nominated movie *Seabiscuit* in 2003.

The Expert Says...

"Seabiscuit was a most unlikely champion — a down-on-his-luck horse whose looks didn't inspire confidence in anyone — except for the people who mattered most."

— Joan Mondale, official representative of the National Trust for Historic Preservation

8 7 6

Seabiscuit IMMORTALIZED

This report details how Seabiscuit was honored for all time.

A life-sized bronze statue of Seabiscuit was officially unveiled on June 23, 2007, at Ridgewood Ranch in Willits, California. This ranch is where the legendary horse spent his final racing years and his retirement. Statue makers crafted the 2007 replica from the mold of an original statue sculpted more than 60 years earlier.

Two statues of Seabiscuit were cast in 1940 and 1941 while the horse was still alive. The first statue was originally displayed at Ridgewood Ranch, but was donated to the National Museum of Racing and Hall of Fame in Saratoga Springs, New York. Seabiscuit himself unveiled the second statue in 1941 at Santa Anita Park in Arcadia, California, where it remains to this day. The inscription reads the same for all three statues:

Biscuit's courage, honesty, and physical prowess definitely place him among the Thoroughbred immortals of turf history. He had intelligence and understanding almost spiritual in quality.

This statue of Seabiscuit is displayed on the grounds of Santa Anita Racetrack in southern California.

Quick Fact

Seabiscuit retired from racing on April 10, 1940. He was inducted into the National Museum of Racing and Hall of Fame in 1958.

Take Note

Seabiscuit amazed the horse-racing world when he started to win races. At #2 on our list, he almost wasn't even given a chance because of his physical appearance and unusual habits. Starting out slowly in his early career, there was no stopping Seabiscuit once he teamed up with owner Charles Howard, trainer Tom Smith, and jockey Red Pollard. Always the smaller, underestimated competitor, it was Seabiscuit's strong spirit that pushed him to victory.

• Like James Braddock, Seabiscuit was a symbol of hope to people during the Great Depression. Compare their two stories and make a list of their similarities.

5   4   3   **2**   1

WUJCIAK
66

77

45

Daniel "Rudy" Ruettiger (#45)
suited up for the game against
Georgia Tech.

DY" RUETTIGER

RUDY-PHOTO COURTESY OF RUDYINTERNATIONAL.COM

SPORT: Football

ONE SHINING MOMENT: Sacked the opposing team's quarterback in the final seconds of his first and only game as a Notre Dame football player

GOING THE DISTANCE: Overcame his small size and limited athletic ability to make the Notre Dame team

On November 8, 1975, the Notre Dame Fighting Irish were playing against Georgia Tech. No one was prepared for what was about to happen when Daniel "Rudy" Ruettiger, a walk-on, stepped onto the field. Rudy entered the game with less than 30 seconds left on the clock and played the last two downs of the game — the only two downs of his entire Notre Dame football career. On the game's final play, he surprised everyone by sacking the opposing team's quarterback.

RU-DY! RU-DY! The chants began to echo throughout Notre Dame Stadium. Rudy was being congratulated by his teammates, coaches, and fans. To this day, Rudy is the only Notre Dame football player to have the honor of being carried off the field by his teammates.

The story of how Rudy became a sports legend goes far beyond the details of that one game. Rudy's determination, perseverance, and sheer will have won him the admiration of fans worldwide.

---

walk-on: *athlete who becomes part of a team without being recruited or awarded an athletic scholarship*
downs: *four chances a team on offense has to gain 10 yards*
sacking: *tackling a player before he or she can pass the ball*

DANIEL 'RUDY' RUETTIGER

AGAINST THE ODDS

Daniel "Rudy" Ruettiger was born in 1948 in Joliet, Illinois. He was the third of 14 children. In high school, Rudy dreamed of playing football for his favorite team — the legendary Fighting Irish. After high school, Rudy spent some time in the navy and worked in a power plant. He eventually enrolled at Holy Cross College in South Bend, Indiana — right across the street from Notre Dame. Rudy spent two years trying to transfer to Notre Dame and was rejected three times. After tests discovered Rudy had dyslexia, he found a way to work with his learning disability. He was finally accepted to Notre Dame in the fall of 1974.

---

dyslexia: *difficulty with reading and writing because of a tendency to reverse letters and words*

? How do you think getting accepted to Notre Dame affected Rudy's self-esteem? How do you think self-esteem helps a person to succeed?

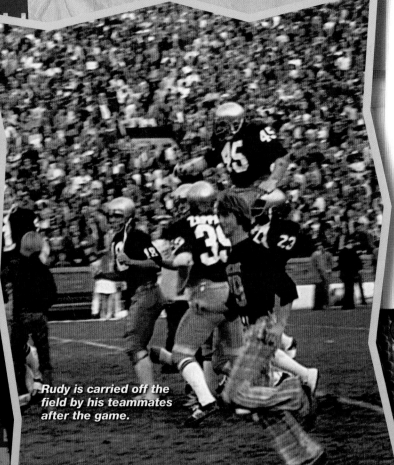

Rudy is carried off the field by his teammates after the game.

GLORY DAYS

Getting into Notre Dame was only half of Rudy's battle. He still dreamed of playing football for the Fighting Irish. At 5'7" and 165 pounds, that wasn't going to be an easy task. But he was persistent and made the team's practice squad. Despite his obvious lack of size or skill, Rudy played with such heart that it earned him the respect of his teammates and coaches. That determination paid off when Rudy was sent in for the final moments of a game against Georgia Tech. On the second of the only two downs he ever played for Notre Dame, he sacked the Georgia Tech quarterback and was carried off the field by his teammates.

Quick Fact

When Rudy played in the Georgia Tech game, his name was not on the jersey that he wore because it was a last minute decision to have him suit up.

INSPIRING LEGACY

Rudy's story was told in the 1993 film *Rudy*. Audiences were entertained and inspired by his amazing tale of grit, determination, and the power of the human spirit. Rudy has been awarded an honorary doctorate from Holy Cross, keys to numerous American cities, and recognition from the White House. Rudy continues to spread his message of hope through his motivational speaking.

---

practice squad: *group of players whose role is to imitate opponents for the starting players*
doctorate: *degree that requires the highest level of education*

Quick Fact

The real Rudy has a cameo in the movie. He is a fan in the stands during the game where he made his famous tackle. He is sitting right behind Ned Beatty, the actor who plays his dad in the movie. Beatty actually tugs on Rudy's shirt when everyone is cheering.

THE LITTLE GUY WITH A BIG DREAM

This interview gets up close and personal with the legend himself — Daniel "Rudy" Ruettiger.

Q: Have you always liked football? Did you play other sports too?

A: Yes. As a small child I would watch the Notre Dame games on TV with my dad and my brothers. I also loved baseball, boxing, wrestling, and waterskiing. I was a championship boxer at Notre Dame.

Q: What impact does the movie have on people?

A: The message definitely changes lives. When I speak, so many people come up to me and tell me how the movie has impacted their life. A dad told me how his son was inspired to live! His son wanted to quit on life — he gave up on sports and in school and had no other hope. He took his dad to the movie and it moved him! The message moved him to believe in himself again!

The Expert Says...

"He's a great inspiration because when I'm down, that's the first DVD I pop in, and that gets me up again."

— Brian Kajiyama, University of Hawaii graduate assistant football coach

Q: Did you realize that your story could have an impact like this?

A: You see the hope and inspiration when the odds are stacked against you so high. You persevered, and you stuck to the commitment — and look at the rewards you're getting today. That's how I feel. That's the magic of it.

Q: What advice would you give to others who want to pursue a dream?

A: Do what you really want to do. Don't let the words of others hold you back. Take a step toward your dream. As you move closer to your dream, new opportunities will open up for you that you never imagined possible.

Take Note

Rudy didn't let his physical limitations or his learning disability stop him from achieving his dream. Through years of rejection and obstacles, Rudy never gave up. He followed a difficult and often thankless route, but in the end, the result was beyond anything he had ever hoped for. He is truly deserving of the #1 spot.

- What are the common qualities shared by the athletes in this book? What do you think is the most important quality?

RUDY PHOTO—PHOTO COURTESY OF RUDYINTERNATIONAL.COM; ALL OTHER IMAGES—SHUTTERSTOCK

We Thought ...

Here are the criteria we used in ranking the 10 best underdog stories in sports.

The underdog story:
- Featured ordinary people doing extraordinary things
- Showed perseverance and persistence
- Inspired athletes and fans
- Had an unexpected outcome
- Featured athletes who faced great odds, but rose to meet the challenge
- Has endured over a long period of time
- Has been retold in movies or books

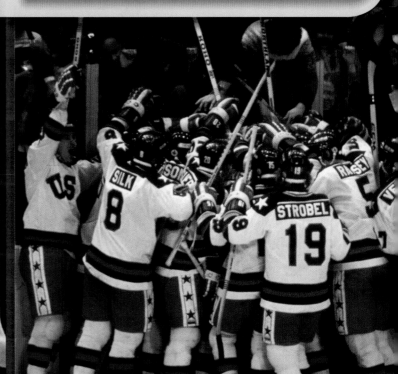

What Do You Think?

1. Do you agree with our ranking? If you don't, try ranking these underdog stories yourself. Justify your ranking with data from your own research and reasoning. You may refer to our criteria, or you may want to draw up your own list of criteria.

2. Here are three other underdog stories that we considered but in the end did not include in our top 10 list: Althea Gibson, Erik Weihenmayer, and the 1954 Milan Indians basketball team.
   • Find out more about these underdog stories. Do you think they should have made our list? Give reasons for your response.
   • Are there any other underdog stories that you think should have made our list? Explain your choices.

Index